GREAT PASTA
SAUCES

SALLY GRIFFITHS

PHOTOGRAPHS BY
SIMON WHEELER

NEW YORK

CONTENTS

INTRODUCTION

In the early Sixties my mother bought a small Italian "casa di campagna" in Calabria. With the house came Anna, much to my mother's surprise and delight, for Anna quickly established herself as confidante, counselor, cook, everything. For me, she soon showed that above all else she was a genius with pasta, and I've enjoyed her recipes ever since.

At that time southern Italy was the unjustly neglected reservoir of honest cooking, although the ingredients in this sunny, sea-encompassed area were extensive. Fruits and vegetables thrived in the strong sunshine and fish and shellfish were plentiful; on the other hand, good beef was scarce. With limited meat resources Anna, in common with other Italian housewives, learned how to stretch and vary the flavor of the pasta sauces and fillings by using generous quantities of fresh local ingredients. As Anna says, "A meal need not be elaborate, it only has to be good."

In my experience pasta dishes are the answer to last-minute suppers and just the thing to set the scene for an elaborate gourmet display. After a long day few of us have either the requisite mood or energy to cope with complicated recipes. With these human frailties in mind I have based my recipes on Anna's expertise. You will find these dishes quick to prepare, easy to cook, delicious to look at and wonderful to eat.

Depending on whether a sauce is oil-based, cheese-based, vegetable- or meat-based, it should be combined with a particular shape of pasta to obtain the correct balance of texture and flavors, and to this end I have outlined a few useful combinations.

Cooking pasta is not difficult, but it has to be just right. In simple question-and-answer form I have explained the basic technique so you can get it perfect every time!

Supermarkets stock a range of Italian products. With this in mind I have compiled a list of ingredients to keep in your pantry so that it is possible to prepare at least 30 of the recipes here without dashing to the stores. I have also included a short, comprehensive list of utensils, one or two of which I find invaluable.

The rest of the book is dedicated to the recipes themselves, and although they are neither long nor complicated I have given a few pages to really simple recipes that require little or no cooking. Thereafter the book is divided into chapters on sauces made with vegetables, eggs and cheese, fish, meat, and game. With each recipe I have suggested an appropriate shape of pasta to complement the sauce, but as there are more than 350 varieties to choose from similar ones often are acceptable.

I have yet to come across anyone who has written about pasta who is not passionate about the subject, and I feel no differently. It has given me enormous pleasure to write this book and I sincerely hope you will enjoy sampling the sauces as much as I did.

UTENSILS

Many of the utensils listed below form part of the everyday kitchen. However, if you don't already have them, it is worth investing in a large colander and, more importantly, a large heavy-based stainless steel pot for cooking pasta.

Large heavy-based stainless steel pot A large pot allows the water to circulate freely and prevents pasta from reabsorbing starch lost during cooking.

Large colander with base and handles Large amounts of pasta drained in a small colander will just slip over the sides, whereas a large colander will enable you to drain, shake, and return the pasta to the warm pot efficiently and quickly.

Garlic press Invest in a sturdy press that empties the pulp easily because you'll be using it a great deal!

Cheese grater You don't need anything elaborate: a simple metal grater is fine.

Citrus juicer Buy one with a guard to prevent the seeds falling into the sauce.

Measuring cups A set of standard cups for dry ingredients and 1-cup and 1-pint measures for liquids are essential.

Measuring spoons Both dry ingredients and liquids are measured in these standard spoons.

Heavy-based skillets Sturdy pans will ensure an even temperature, and they will last for years.

Food processor This is a real time-saver.

Long-handled wooden spoons With these you can stir the pasta in the large pot easily.

Long-handled forks These are invaluable when you are testing long, slippery strands of pasta. There also are wooden pasta "forks"—really paddles with long pegs attached—made just for this purpose.

Parmesan knife The short, sharp blade can pare slices from large pieces of Parmesan.

Pepper grinder or mill Choose one to complement your table setting. Grinders come in wood, stainless steel, or plastic and many attractive colors.

Potato peeler Use it to make curls of Parmesan for salads or decoration.

Small wooden spoons These are less abrasive (and less noisy) than metal ones.

Small saucepans A few small saucepans are invaluable.

Chopping boards They will prevent worksurfaces from becoming damaged or scratched.

Storage jars These are useful for keeping dry pasta once the package has been opened.

Plastic chopping board Use this to chop garlic or any other ingredient with a strong smell.

Long-handled rubber spatula Use it to scrape mixtures down the sides of the blender or food processor.

Knives Really sharp knives make chopping and slicing much easier.

Bowls A good selection of bowls is useful for mixing ingredients.

Pestle and mortar Crushing peppercorns or small amounts of herbs in a mortar is a simple yet effective way of releasing the full flavor of the ingredient.

Slotted spoon This is useful for lifting and draining cooked stuffed pasta shapes.

THE KITCHEN PANTRY

Although fresh produce is generally considered superior, many canned goods are perfectly acceptable for pasta sauces. Most of the ingredients listed below are available in supermarkets. Alternatively, head for a good Italian grocery store and indulge.

Dried pasta

Keep a variety of different shapes and sizes such as: capelli d'angelo, spaghetti, linguine or trenette, bucatini, fettuccine, tagliatelle, fusilli, farfalle, conchiglie, penne, rigatoni, and tortellini.

General ingredients

Anchovies, sardines, canned salmon, canned tuna, canned clams, mustard, jars or cans of roasted peppers or pimientos, green olives, pitted black olives, capers, canned beans such as flageolet, dried porcini, sun-dried tomatoes (packed dry or in olive oil), canned tomatoes (at least 4 cans), natural, not seasoned, dry bread crumbs, red and white wine

Nuts and seeds

Store in tightly sealed containers or they will become rancid and soft.

Pine nuts, sliced almonds, walnuts, poppy seeds

Oils and vinegars

Keep well-sealed, away from the light.

Extra virgin olive oil, truffle oil, walnut or hazelnut oil, chili oil, light olive oil (for frying), balsamic vinegar, white wine vinegar

Pastes

To keep paste in jars fresh, pour a thin layer of olive oil over the surface each time you remove a spoonful.

Green olive paste, black olive paste, tomato paste; tomato paste in a tube is ideal.

Pepper and salt

Store in a cool, dry place. To prevent salt absorbing moisture, mix with a few grains of rice.

Black peppercorns, sea salt (fine and coarsely ground)

Spices

Store in airtight containers in a cool, dry, dark place.

Hot red pepper flakes, nutmeg, cinnamon, saffron threads

Dried herbs

Store in airtight containers in a cool, dry, dark place.

Marjoram, oregano, tarragon, thyme, rosemary, basil, bay leaves, dill

Fresh herbs

Grow them in a window box or in pretty pots on the window sill.

Basil, cilantro, flat-leaf parsley, chives

Fresh vegetables

Tomatoes, lemons, garlic, onions, shallots, bell peppers, hot chili peppers

Bacon and ham

Prosciutto and pancetta (keep tightly wrapped in the refrigerator)

Dairy

Parmesan and pecorino romano cheese (keep in chunks, tightly wrapped), crème fraîche (keeps longer than ordinary cream), butter, cream, eggs

Frozen ingredients

Green peas, homemade veal, vegetable, chicken, and fish stocks

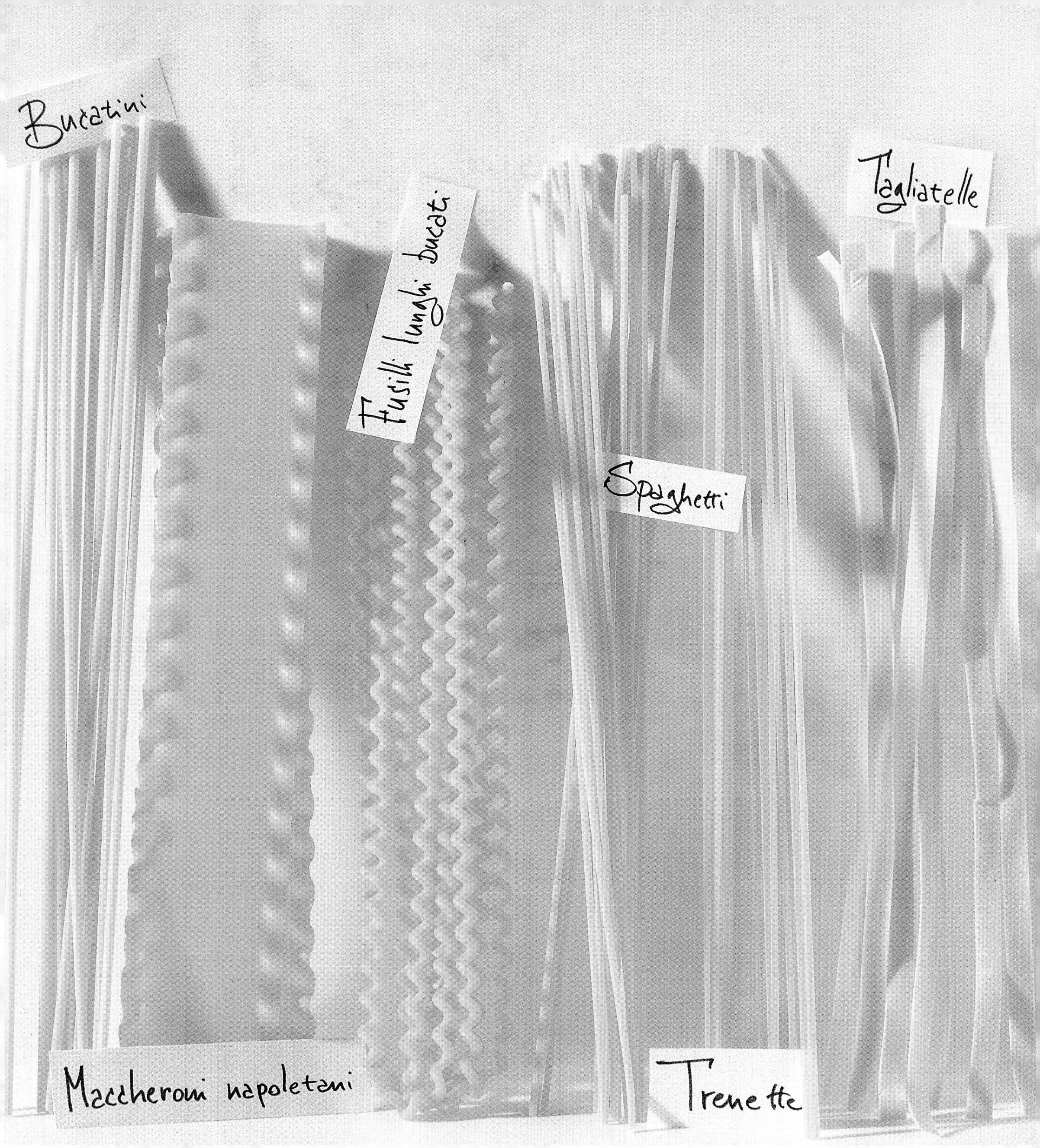

Bucatini

Tagliatelle

Fusilli lunghi bucati

Spaghetti

Maccheroni napoletani

Trenette

PASTA SHAPES

Pasta comes in hundreds of different shapes, and in Italy, the combination of flavor,

texture, and shape is taken very seriously. For example:

Long, round pasta –

such as fedelini, spaghettini, vermicelli, spaghetti, or spaghettoni, needs an olive-oil-based sauce to keep the strands slippery and separate.

Long, flat pasta –

linguine, trenette, fettuccine, tagliatelle, bucatini, tagliolini, lasagnette, noodles, lasagne, and tonnarelli, for example—should be accompanied by richer sauces based on cheese, eggs, and/or cream or ones that contain small pieces of meat such as prosciutto.

Short pasta –

i.e. shaped and tubular—is best served with a juicy sauce that will penetrate into the pasta hollows. Shaped and medium-sized tubular pasta are excellent with vegetable-based sauces, and larger examples, such as penne rigate or macaroni, are ideal in baked dishes or with rich meat sauces.

Filled pasta –

these pasta wrappings may be stuffed with a variety of delicious ingredients. It is best to keep the sauce simple so that it does not overpower the flavor of the filling—a little melted butter and cheese, for example. Ravioli, cannelloni and lasagne are familiar filled pastas.

Tortellini

Lasagne

Tagliarini

Ta...

Fettuccine

Ravioli

Ravioli alla ricotta e

ALL ABOUT PASTA

Beware the pronouncements of any self-styled historian-cum-gastronome who speaks authoritatively of the origins of pasta cuisine, probably citing some esoteric corner of Italy. The simple fact is that nobody knows where or how pasta came our way. What is certain, however, is that pasta occurred, probably spontaneously, in various places. Whatever, whenever, and wherever the origins of pasta, its appetizing flavors have enlivened first Italian and then the Western world's tables ever since.

How many different shapes of pasta are there? The Italians have invented over 350 different shapes of pasta, each one suitable for a certain sauce (see page 13).

Should pasta be served as a first course or a main course? It can be hot, cold, a first course, main course, even a dessert. Italians sometimes serve a small helping of pasta between the antipasto and fish or meat courses.

Is pasta good for you? Pasta contains protein, vitamins, and minerals. It is high in carbohydrates and helps sustain energy.

Is pasta fattening? Pasta on its own is not. It's the accompanying sauce that can send the calories spiraling upward.

Is there an alternative to wheat-based pasta? Try spelt-based pasta (you will find it in healthfood stores). It is low in gluten and can be eaten by anybody with an allergy to wheat.

Which is best, fresh or dried pasta? Neither. Dried and fresh are two distinct but equal categories. Quality is always important, however, and it is important to use a good-quality Italian brand of dried pasta.

How can you tell freshly made pasta? Buy from a store that has a brisk turnover. Fresh pasta should really be cooked the day it is made. Not-quite-fresh pasta will darken in color and begin to shrivel but will swell considerably during cooking and end up a sticky mass.

What type of sauce is served with fresh pasta? A light sauce incorporating cream, butter, cheese, or any ingredient that will be absorbed by the porous surface of the dough.

What is the advantage of dried pasta? It keeps for at least a year and comes in an enormous variety of different shapes and sizes.

Is fresh pasta considered more authentic than dried? No. Fresh pasta is found more often in the north of Italy, whereas in the south dried pasta is more typical, but these are generalities, and it is the dish, not the type of pasta, that determines authenticity.

How do you know which pasta to use with which sauce? As a general rule, long, round pasta is served with oil-based sauces, flat pasta with sauces based on eggs, cheese, cream, or light meats, and shaped and tubular pasta with thicker sauces that can penetrate the hollows.

How long does pasta keep? Dried pasta will keep approximately one year, whereas fresh pasta is best eaten on the day of purchase.

How is dried pasta made? The basic dough is made with finely ground durum wheat and water (some include eggs). Make sure you buy a good Italian brand because inferior makes sometimes split during cooking —look out for the words durum wheat or pura semolina on the package.

What is the difference between "fresh pasta" found in supermarkets, and homemade pasta? Because supermarket brands are mass-produced using machinery, they do not really compare with homemade pasta, made by hand, which has a lightness and delicacy of its own.

What is durum wheat flour? Durum wheat is grown mostly in Canada and the United States. When ground to flour it gives the pasta its firm texture. The durum wheat grown in Italy is called semolina.

What is the difference between pasta made with eggs and without eggs? Pasta made with eggs is slightly richer in taste and color. Eggs add protein, and give the pasta a more tender texture.

COOKING PASTA

At what stage do you cook the pasta? Cook it just before serving.

How much pasta per person? Much depends on your appetite. The following amounts are for four people.

As a first course :

Dried pasta: 6–8 ounces

Fresh pasta: 1–1 1/2 pounds

As a main course:

Dried pasta: 1 pound

Fresh pasta: 2 pounds

How do you cook pasta? Bring a large pot of water to a boil, add salt and then the pasta, and stir well. Put the lid on the pot until the water returns to boiling, then remove it. Stir the pasta several times during the cooking process. To make sure the pasta does not overcook, test it once or twice a minute or two before the manufacturer's recommended cooking time is up. Then toss with the sauce and serve immediately.

For cold pasta, cook as above, then drain and toss with a little olive oil. Allow to cool at room temperature.

Which kind of pot is best for cooking pasta? To make sure pasta cooks evenly and does not stick together, use a heavy-based pot that is large enough to allow the water to circulate around the pasta and remain at a constant temperature.

How much water do you need? During the cooking process pasta absorbs water and loses starch. If there is insufficient water in the pot, the pasta will reabsorb the starch. Work on a ratio of 1 quart of water to 3 1/2 ounces of pasta.

Should the water be salted? Yes, otherwise the pasta will taste rather bland. Add a generous pinch or two of salt after the water boils.

How do you prevent pasta sticking to the pot? As soon as you put the pasta into boiling water, stir well, then stir again several times during the cooking process. Oil should not be added.

How long does pasta take to cook? Fresh pasta cooks in approximately 2–3 minutes (stuffed pasta takes a little longer), whereas dried pasta can take from 4 to 15 minutes, depending on its size and shape.

How can you tell when pasta is cooked? Using a fork, take out a piece of pasta once or twice before the recommended cooking time is up and test. Pasta should be cooked al dente, which means firm to the bite.

Can you overcook pasta? Pasta becomes a soft, sticky mass if cooked too long. The only thing to do is throw it away and start again!

Should you use a strainer or a colander to drain pasta? As soon the pasta is cooked, tip it into a large colander, give a few shakes, and return the pasta to the pot or put it in a preheated dish. Do not over-drain—pasta should be slippery so that the sauce coats it properly. To drain stuffed pasta, lift it out of the water with a slotted spoon.

Do you pour cold water over pasta after draining it? No. It would remove the coating of starch and cool it down. Toss pasta and sauce together immediately.

When do you add the sauce to the pasta? As soon as the pasta is drained, toss it with the sauce. For stuffed pasta, which might break if tossed, either pour the sauce into a dish and lay the pasta on top or gently spoon the sauce over the pasta.

How much sauce should be served with pasta? Not too much. The sauce is only intended to coat the pasta; the pasta should not swim around in it.

Are there any traditional accompaniments to serve with pasta? Grated Parmesan cheese is sprinkled over many pasta dishes just before eating, but generally not those with fish-based sauces. Other garnishes include freshly ground black pepper, pecorino romano cheese, toasted pine nuts (see below), and freshly chopped herbs depending on the dish.

HOW TO:

Toast nuts and seeds Toss them around in a hot, dry skillet until they are lightly browned.

Peel tomatoes Put the tomatoes in a large bowl of boiling water and let stand for 1–2 minutes. Remove, and the skin will peel off easily.

Peel peppers Roast peppers in a preheated 400°F oven until the skins become blistered and black, 25–30 minutes. Remove, put them in a plastic bag, seal, let cool, and then peel off the skin.

Sweat To "sweat" means sauté for a few minutes until the ingredients become soft and transparent.

PESTO

All recipes are for four people. Bursting with flavor, these aromatic sauces have a wonderful, voluptuous consistency. Serve with spaghetti or a long, flat pasta such as trenette, tagliatelle, or fettuccine. (Delicious with hot or cold pasta.)

- Pesto can be kept 1 week in an airtight container in the refrigerator.
- Too much blending will ruin the lovely nutty texture.

ARUGULA PESTO

2/3 cup pine nuts
2 ounces fresh arugula, with stems
1 1/2–2 cloves garlic, peeled and crushed with a garlic press
1/2 cup freshly grated Parmesan cheese
1 tablespoon lemon juice

Salt
2/3 cup extra virgin olive oil
TO FINISH
Freshly ground black pepper
1/3 cup pine nuts, toasted (see page 17)
Freshly grated Parmesan cheese

Place all the ingredients, except the oil, in a food processor and blend until roughly chopped, about 30 seconds. Then slowly pour in the oil, and blend until smooth.

Toss with pasta, season with pepper, and sprinkle with toasted pine nuts and Parmesan.

- Try walnut pieces instead of pine nuts.
- Use raw baby spinach leaves instead of arugula.
- If the sauce is too dry, add more oil.

BASIL PESTO

2 ounces fresh basil leaves
(about 1 1/3 cups loosely packed)
1 clove garlic, peeled and crushed with a garlic press
1 tablespoon pine nuts

6 tablespoons extra virgin olive oil
TO FINISH
Salt and freshly ground black pepper
1/4 cup freshly grated Parmesan cheese

Put all the ingredients, except the oil, in a food processor and blend until roughly chopped, about 30 seconds. Then slowly pour in the oil and blend until smooth.

Toss with pasta, season, and sprinkle with Parmesan.

- If the sauce is too dry, add more oil and blend for a few seconds.

PARSLEY AND HAZELNUT PESTO

2 ounces fresh parsley without stems
(about 1 cup)
1/4 cup freshly grated Parmesan cheese
2 cloves garlic, peeled and crushed with a garlic press
1 tablespoon lemon juice

2 tablespoons chopped hazelnuts
6 tablespoons hazelnut oil
6 tablespoons peanut oil
TO FINISH
Salt and freshly ground black pepper
Freshly grated Parmesan cheese

Make as for Basil Pesto.

SPINACH AND WALNUT PESTO

2 ounces baby spinach leaves
2 heaping tablespoons walnut pieces
2 1/2 tablespoons freshly grated Parmesan cheese
1 1/2 tablespoons lemon juice
2 cloves garlic, peeled and crushed with a garlic press

Salt
1 cup extra virgin olive oil
TO FINISH
Salt and freshly ground black pepper
Freshly grated Parmesan cheese

Make as for Basil Pesto.

SORREL PESTO

1/4 pound sorrel
2/3 cup pine nuts, toasted (see page 17)
1/2 cup freshly grated Parmesan cheese
2 tablespoons extra virgin olive oil

TO FINISH
Salt and freshly ground black pepper
Freshly grated Parmesan cheese

Make as for Basil Pesto.

SUN-DRIED TOMATO PESTO

2 tablespoons chopped sun-dried tomatoes, reconstituted in warm water or drained of oil
2 heaping tablespoons fresh parsley without stems
2 heaping tablespoons pitted black olives
3/4 cup pine nuts
2 shallots, chopped

2 cloves garlic, peeled and crushed with a garlic press
1 tablespoon lemon juice
Salt
1/4 cup extra virgin olive oil
TO FINISH
Salt and freshly ground black pepper
Freshly grated Parmesan cheese

Make as for Basil Pesto.

MIXED HERB PESTO

4 ounces fresh parsley without stems
1/2 ounce fresh basil leaves
(about 1/3 cup loosely packed)
1 can (2 ounces) anchovies, drained and rinsed
3 tablespoons capers
2 cloves garlic, peeled and crushed with a garlic press

1 tablespoon chopped onion
2/3 cup fresh bread crumbs
3 tablespoons lemon juice
7 tablespoons extra virgin olive oil
TO FINISH
Salt and freshly ground black pepper
Freshly grated Parmesan cheese

Make as for Basil Pesto.

CILANTRO PESTO

2 ounces fresh cilantro leaves (about 1 cup)
1 tablespoon pine nuts
1/2–1 teaspoon dried hot red pepper flakes
1 tablespoon lemon juice

1/2 cup extra virgin olive oil
TO FINISH
Salt and freshly ground black pepper
Freshly grated Parmesan cheese

Make as for Basil Pesto.

Right: Arugula Pesto

OIL AND BUTTER BASED SAUCES

All recipes are for four people.

Oil- and butter-based sauces served with long round pasta, a delicious salad, and plenty of fresh bread make perfect impromptu

meals. Straight from the pantry, they are quick and easy to make and the flavors of the ingredients are beautifully accentuated.

Oil- and butter-based sauces are particularly suited to stuffed pastas.

OIL AND GARLIC

1/2 cup extra virgin olive oil
2 cloves garlic, peeled and minced
Salt and freshly ground black pepper
Freshly grated Parmesan cheese

In a small pan over a low heat, barely warm the olive oil, then add the garlic and warm gently for 30 seconds longer. Toss the garlic oil with hot pasta, season, and sprinkle with Parmesan.

OIL, GARLIC, AND HERB

1/2 cup extra virgin olive oil
2 cloves garlic, peeled and minced
1 tablespoon minced fresh parsley
1 heaping tablespoon fresh basil leaves torn in strips
Salt and freshly ground black pepper
Freshly grated Parmesan cheese

In a small pan over a low heat, barely warm the olive oil, then add the garlic and warm gently for a further 30 seconds. Toss the garlic oil and herbs with hot pasta, mixing together well. Season and sprinkle with Parmesan.

• As an alternative, replace the parsley and basil with 2 tablespoons chopped fresh chives or oregano.

• Add a handful of toasted pine nuts (see page 17) with the herbs for a crunchier texture.

OIL AND CILANTRO

1/2 cup extra virgin olive oil
1 clove garlic, peeled and minced
2 tablespoons chopped fresh cilantro
Salt and freshly ground black pepper
Freshly grated Parmesan cheese

In a small pan over a low heat, barely warm the olive oil, then add garlic and warm gently for a further 30 seconds. Toss the garlic oil and cilantro with hot pasta, season, and sprinkle with Parmesan.

TRUFFLE OIL

2 tablespoons truffle oil
Salt and freshly ground black pepper
Freshly grated Parmesan cheese

In a small heavy-based pan, gently warm the oil, then toss with hot pasta, season, and sprinkle with Parmesan.

• Excellent with stuffed pasta such as ravioli.

OIL, CHILI, AND GARLIC

1/2 cup extra virgin olive oil
1 clove garlic, peeled and crushed with a garlic press
2 teaspoons dried hot red pepper flakes

Heat the oil in a small, heavy-based pan over a medium heat, add the garlic, and cook until golden, about 30 seconds. Remove the garlic with a slotted spoon and discard. Add the hot pepper flakes to the garlic-flavored oil and toss with hot pasta. Season, and add a little more oil if desired.

BUTTER AND PARMESAN

1 stick (1/2 cup) butter
1/4 cup freshly grated Parmesan cheese
Freshly ground black pepper

Gently melt the butter in a small saucepan over a low heat, then toss with hot pasta. Stir in the Parmesan and season with pepper.

CHIVE BUTTER

1 stick (1/2 cup) butter
1/3 cup chopped fresh chives
Salt and freshly ground black pepper
Freshly grated Parmesan cheese

Melt the butter in a small saucepan over a low heat. Add the chives, stir, and toss with hot pasta. Season and sprinkle with Parmesan.

BUTTER AND BROWNED GARLIC

1 stick (1/2 cup) butter
3–4 cloves garlic, peeled and crushed with a garlic press
Freshly ground black pepper
1 cup freshly grated Parmesan cheese

In a heavy-based pan, heat the butter until it starts to foam. Add the garlic and, stirring constantly, cook until golden brown, about 1–2 minutes. Toss with hot pasta, season with pepper, and stir in the Parmesan.

BUTTER AND TOASTED POPPY SEED

1 stick (1/2 cup) butter
3 tablespoons poppy seeds, toasted (see page 17)
Salt and freshly ground black pepper
Freshly grated Parmesan cheese

Gently melt the butter in a small saucepan over a low heat, then toss with hot pasta. Add the poppy seeds and mix together well. Season and sprinkle with Parmesan.

Left: Oil, Chili, and Garlic

CREAM, EGG, AND CHEESE SAUCES

All recipes are for four people.

CREAM AND BLACK OLIVE SAUCE

The dramatic combination of black and white makes this a wonderful sauce for a dinner party. Try it with fettuccine, and a crisp green salad.

1/4 cup pitted black olives
Leaves stripped from 2 sprigs fresh thyme
1 teaspoon dried herbes de Provence
4 baby gherkins or cornichons
1 clove garlic, peeled
1 tablespoon olive oil
3 tablespoons butter
2 1/2 cups light cream or crème fraîche

Put the olives, thyme, herbes de Provence, gherkins, garlic, and olive oil in a food processor and blend to a paste. Melt the butter in a small saucepan over a low heat, then add the paste and stir together well. Stir in the cream and cook until the sauce has reduced a little, about 5 minutes.

Toss with hot pasta and serve.

CARBONARA SAUCE

Eggs with bacon is a tried and tested favorite. Serve this sauce with bucatini or spaghetti, and a tomato salad.

4 tablespoons butter or olive oil
1/4 pound pancetta or smoked bacon, any rind removed, cut in small strips
4 egg yolks
1 tablespoon milk
1/3 cup freshly grated pecorino romano cheese
Salt and freshly ground black pepper
Freshly grated Parmesan cheese

Heat the butter or oil in a heavy-based pan over a low heat and fry the pancetta until lightly browned, about 10 minutes. (If using bacon, omit the butter or oil.) Remove the pancetta or bacon with a slotted spoon and place in a deep, warm bowl. Put the egg yolks, milk, and pecorino romano in a small bowl and lightly beat with a fork to mix. Pour the mixture over the bacon, add the hot pasta, and toss together well. Season, and sprinkle with grated Parmesan.

EGG AND HERB SAUCE

One of the simplest yet most sophisticated sauces in the book. Serve with pasta shells or fusilli.

2 tablespoons chopped fresh parsley
2 tablespoons chopped fresh basil
2 tablespoons chopped fresh chervil
2 tablespoons chopped fresh chives
1 teaspoon capers, chopped
6 hard-boiled egg yolks, cooled and pressed through a fine strainer
6 tablespoons extra virgin olive oil
Salt and freshly ground black pepper

Mix together all the ingredients in a bowl, season, and toss with hot pasta.

• This can also be served with cold pasta.

CREAM, PORCINI, AND SHERRY SAUCE

This ambrosial sauce is irresistible! Serve with a long, flat pasta such as pappardelle, and an arugula salad.

3/4 ounce dried porcini
6 tablespoons sherry
6 tablespoons madeira
3 tablespoons butter
2 cloves garlic, peeled and minced
2 shallots, minced
1 1/2 cups heavy cream
Salt and freshly ground black pepper
1 1/2 tablespoons chopped fresh chives

Soak the porcini in the sherry and madeira for 15 minutes, then drain, taking care to leave any grit at the bottom of the bowl, and reserve the liquid.

Melt the butter in a heavy-based pan over a medium heat and gently fry the garlic and shallots for 3 minutes. Add the porcini and cook for 1 minute. Turn up the heat and stir in the cream and reserved soaking liquid. Cook until the sauce is creamy and thick, about 5 minutes.

Season, toss with hot pasta, and sprinkle with chives.

BLUE CHEESE AND BROCCOLI SAUCE WITH TOASTED NUTS

The shapes, colors, and textures in this wonderful sauce complement each other beautifully. Serve with a large pasta shape such as penne rigate, and plenty of bread to mop up the sauce.

1/2 pound small broccoli florets
1 tablespoon olive oil
1 small onion, minced
2/3 cup dry white wine
1/4 cup heavy cream
Salt and freshly ground black pepper
1/4 pound cambozola, or other creamy blue cheese, chopped in small pieces
2 tablespoons sliced almonds, toasted (see page 17)

Cook the broccoli in salted boiling water for 3–4 minutes. Drain and put aside in a warm bowl.

Heat the oil in a heavy-based pan and gently fry the onion for 3 minutes. Add the wine and cream, bring to a boil, and reduce a little, then season and stir in the cheese.

Toss the broccoli with hot pasta, then gently mix in the sauce. Sprinkle with the almonds and serve.

Right: Carbonara Sauce

Stilton, red wine, and walnut sauce

Serve this rich, velvety sauce with pappardelle, and a salad of radicchio, Belgian endive, and celery.

1 1/2 cups heavy cream
6 tablespoons red wine or port wine
3/4 pound stilton cheese, crumbled
Salt and freshly ground black pepper

1 1/4 cups walnut pieces, toasted
(see page 17) and chopped
4–6 tablespoons chopped fresh parsley

Put the cream in a large saucepan and bring to a boil. Add the red wine or port, reduce the heat, and simmer for 5 minutes. Add the stilton and cook gently until the cheese has melted and the sauce thickens, about 3 minutes. Season, toss with hot pasta, and sprinkle with walnuts and parsley.

Mozzarella, tomato, and chili sauce

The combination of red and white makes this an eye-catching sauce. Serve with fusilli, and some hot Italian bread.

3 tablespoons olive oil
4 cloves garlic, minced
1 fresh hot red chili pepper,
seeded and chopped

1 pound ripe tomatoes, peeled
(see page 17), seeded, and chopped
Salt and freshly ground black pepper
1/4 pound mozzarella cheese,
cut in 1/2-inch squares

Put the oil in a heavy-based pan and gently fry the garlic and chili over a medium heat for 1 minute (be careful not to burn the garlic). Turn up the heat, add the tomatoes, and season. Cook for 4 minutes, stirring occasionally. Toss the sauce and mozzarella with hot pasta and serve at once.

Dolcelatte and walnut sauce

This creamy sauce has a lovely nutty texture. Serve with farfalle, a Belgian endive salad, and plenty of Italian bread to mop up the sauce.

1/2 cup heavy cream
6 ounces dolcelatte
(creamy gorgonzola) cheese
1/2 cup walnut pieces

Salt and freshly ground black pepper
1 heaping tablespoon fresh basil leaves
torn in strips

Gently heat the cream and cheese in a heavy-based pan over a medium heat, stirring constantly. When melted and smooth, add the nuts and mix together well. Season. Remove from the heat, stir in the basil, and toss with hot pasta.

• Try roughly chopped pecans instead of walnuts.

Ricotta and tomato sauce

This delicate sauce is excellent for a light supper dish. Serve with linguine, and a salad of arugula and freshly shaved pecorino romano cheese.

1/3 cup extra virgin olive oil
4 green onions, chopped, or
1/3 cup chopped fresh chives
1/2 pound (1 cup) ricotta cheese, crumbled
1/4 cup freshly grated Parmesan cheese,
plus more for serving

4 ripe tomatoes, peeled (see page 17),
seeded, and diced
1/2 cup fresh basil leaves torn in strips
Salt and freshly ground black pepper

Heat the oil in a heavy-based pan over a very low heat. Add the green onions or chives, ricotta, and Parmesan and mix together well. Cook for 1 minute, then stir in tomatoes, basil, and seasoning. As soon as the sauce start to warm, remove from the heat, toss with hot pasta, and sprinkle with more Parmesan.

Ricotta and butter sauce

A light, fluffy sauce, this is excellent with tagliatelle, and a crisp green salad.

1 stick (1/2 cup) butter
1 1/4 pounds (2 1/2 cups)
ricotta cheese, crumbled

Salt
Mixed (4-colored) peppercorns,
freshly ground

Melt the butter in a small saucepan over a medium heat, and pour over hot pasta. Sprinkle the ricotta over the top, season with salt, and toss well. Serve with freshly ground multicolored peppercorns.

Mascarpone and walnut sauce

Creamy and crunchy, this marvelous sauce has a good combination of textures and flavors. Serve with large penne, and a bacon and spinach salad.

4 tablespoons butter
1 clove garlic, peeled and crushed
with a garlic press
1 3/4 cups walnut pieces

9 ounces (1 cup + 2 tablespoons)
mascarpone cheese
1/2 cup freshly grated Parmesan cheese
Salt and freshly ground black pepper

Melt the butter in a heavy-based pan and fry the garlic over a medium heat until golden, about 30 seconds. Add the walnuts and gently toss around for 3–4 minutes. Then stir in the mascarpone and keep stirring until it has completely melted. Fold in the Parmesan, season, and toss with hot pasta.

Egg and caper sauce

Straight out of the pantry! Try this egg-based sauce with spaghettini or tagliolini.

2 tablespoons butter, softened
3 jumbo eggs, lightly beaten
1 cup freshly grated pecorino romano cheese

1 tablespoon capers, drained and rinsed
1 tablespoon chopped fresh parsley
Salt and freshly ground black pepper

Put all the ingredients in a bowl and mix together well. Season and toss with hot pasta.

Left: Blue Cheese and Broccoli Sauce with Toasted Nuts

CREAM AND LEMON SAUCE

The tangy flavor of lemon adds a perfect contrast in this delicate, creamy sauce. Serve with festoni, and a radicchio salad.

2 tablespoons butter
1 cup heavy cream
2 tablespoons grated lemon zest

2 tablespoons freshly grated Parmesan cheese
1 tablespoon pine nuts, toasted (see page 17)
Salt and freshly ground black pepper

Place the butter, cream, and lemon zest in a small saucepan and bring to a boil. Once the liquid has reached boiling point, lower the heat, stir in the Parmesan, and sprinkle with the pine nuts. Season and toss with hot pasta.

RICOTTA AND FRESH HERB SAUCE

The pungent aroma of fresh herbs and the subtle flavor of ricotta makes this sauce the perfect choice for a light supper dish. Serve with conchiglie, and a spinach salad.

1 pound (2 cups) ricotta cheese
2 tablespoons freshly grated Parmesan cheese
2 tablespoons chopped fresh flat-leaf parsley
2 tablespoons chopped fresh basil

2 tablespoons chopped fresh chives
2 tablespoons chopped fresh oregano
Salt and freshly ground black pepper

Mix all the ingredients in a bowl, season, and fold into hot pasta.

• This sauce can also be served with cold pasta.

CREME FRAICHE AND SUN-DRIED TOMATO SAUCE

Evoking memories of hot sunny days, this simple sauce can be served with penne or rigatoni, and a salad of chicory, Belgian endive, and fresh basil.

1 cup crème fraîche
1/3 cup sun-dried tomato paste

6 sun-dried tomatoes, reconstituted in warm water or drained of oil, then cut in thin strips
Freshly ground black pepper

Combine the crème fraîche and tomato paste and mix together well. Stir in the sun-dried tomatoes, season, and toss with hot pasta.

• This sauce can also be served with cold pasta or as a side dish on its own.

GOAT CHEESE AND TOMATO SAUCE

Tastes of the Mediterranean! Serve this summery sauce with tagliatelle, and a salad of tomatoes, onion, and juicy black olives.

1 1/2 pounds ripe tomatoes, peeled (see page 17), seeded, and chopped
1/3 cup coarsely chopped fresh basil

5 ounces fresh goat cheese, crumbled
6 tablespoons extra virgin olive oil
Salt and freshly ground black pepper

Combine all the ingredients in a large bowl, season, and toss with hot pasta.

• Goat cheese with herbs and garlic is a lovely alternative to plain goat cheese.

• This sauce can also be served as a dish on its own.

THREE CHEESE SAUCE

Throw this impressive sauce together in a flash. Serve with green tagliatelle or fettuccine, and a radicchio salad.

1 1/2 tablespoons butter
2 ounces dolcelatte or gorgonzola cheese, cut in small cubes
1/4 pound (1/2 cup) mascarpone cheese

3/4 cup freshly grated Parmesan cheese
1/4 teaspoon grated nutmeg
10 large leaves fresh basil, torn in strips

Melt the butter in a heavy-based saucepan over a medium heat. Add the cheeses and stir to mix together well. Toss with hot pasta and sprinkle with nutmeg and basil.

• Add a tablespoon of toasted sliced almonds or chopped walnuts for a crunchier texture.

Right: *Three Cheese Sauce*

VEGETABLE SAUCES

All recipes are for four people.

QUICK TOMATO SAUCE WITH CREAM AND SUN-DRIED TOMATOES

Quick and easy, this wonderful sauce is bursting with flavor. Serve with penne, and a green bean salad.

1 tablespoon olive oil
1 clove garlic, peeled and crushed with a garlic press
1 can (16 ounces) tomatoes, drained
1 teaspoon tomato paste

1/2 cup heavy cream
1 tablespoon minced sun-dried tomatoes, reconstituted in warm water or drained of oil
1 teaspoon chopped fresh flat-leaf parsley
Salt and freshly ground black pepper

Heat the oil in a heavy-based pan and fry the garlic until pale golden, about 30 seconds. Add the tomatoes, turn up the heat, and cook for 5 minutes, mashing them with a spoon. Then lower the heat and stir in the tomato paste. Add the cream and sun-dried tomatoes and simmer gently for a further 3 minutes.

Fold in the parsley, season, and toss with hot pasta.

BLACK OLIVE AND CHILI SAUCE

The provocative flavor of olives is accentuated by marinating them overnight. Serve with linguine, and a tomato salad.

• Remember to marinate the olives overnight.

5 tablespoons extra virgin olive oil
1 1/3 cups chopped black olives
1/2 teaspoon dried hot red pepper flakes

2 cloves garlic, peeled and minced
1 tablespoon chopped fresh parsley
Salt and freshly ground black pepper

Mix 2 tablespoons of the oil with the olives, hot pepper flakes, and garlic in a bowl and let marinate overnight.

The next day, heat the remaining oil in a heavy-based pan and add the marinated olive mixture, parsley, and a little salt. Simmer gently for 5 minutes. Season and toss with hot pasta.

• This sauce can also be served with cold pasta.

OYSTER MUSHROOM SAUCE

High in flavor, low in calories. Serve with capelli d'angeli, and a watercress and orange salad.

4 tablespoons sesame oil
1 leek, cut lengthwise in very fine strips
12 green onions, green ends only, chopped
1 clove garlic, peeled and crushed with a garlic press
2 tablespoons soy sauce
1/2 cup fresh orange juice
1/2-inch strip lemon zest

1/2 teaspoon sugar
1 teaspoon sherry vinegar
1/4 teaspoon five spice powder (or ground galangal)
1/4 pound oyster mushrooms
TO FINISH
Salt and freshly ground black pepper
2 tablespoons sesame seeds, toasted (see page 17)

Heat 2 tablespoons of the sesame oil in a skillet, add the leeks, and, turning constantly, fry until the strips become dark brown and crispy. Remove with a slotted spoon, drain on paper towels, and set aside.

Heat the remaining sesame oil in a large skillet and gently fry the green onions and garlic for 1–2 minutes. Add the soy sauce, orange juice, lemon zest, sugar, and vinegar and bring to a boil. Cook for 2–3 minutes, then add the five spice powder (or ground galangal) and oyster mushrooms and mix together over a medium heat for 1 minute.

Toss with hot pasta, season, and sprinkle with toasted sesame seeds. Serve the crispy leeks on the side.

• This sauce can also be served with cold pasta.

MUSHROOM SAUCE WITH DRIED PORCINI

Dried porcini have a wonderful woody flavor and are justifiably considered a great delicacy. Serve this sauce with tagliatelle, a crisp green salad, and focaccia bread.

1 ounce dried porcini
2/3 cup dry white wine
1 stick (1/2 cup) butter
1 onion, chopped
1 clove garlic, peeled and crushed
with a garlic press
1 tablespoon chopped fresh parsley
1 heaping tablespoon fresh basil leaves
torn in strips

1 teaspoon tomato paste
1 pound mixed fresh mushrooms (button,
oyster, and portobello), roughly chopped,
except the oyster mushrooms
Salt and freshly ground black pepper
1 tablespoon flour
1/2 cup meat stock, preferably homemade
1 teaspoon Dijon mustard
Freshly grated Parmesan cheese

Put the dried porcini in a bowl, cover with hot water, and let soak for 30 minutes. Drain, taking care to leave any grit from the porcini at the bottom of the bowl. Reserve 1/2 cup of the liquid.

In a small saucepan heat the wine and simmer for 4 minutes, then set aside.

Melt half the butter in a heavy-based pan and gently cook the onion until soft but not browned. Add the garlic and herbs and cook for 1 minute, then add the tomato paste and cook for a further 30 seconds. Stir in the drained porcini and sauté for 5 minutes, then add the fresh mushrooms and cook over a medium heat for 5 minutes, turning the mushrooms regularly. Season, lower the heat, and cook for another 5 minutes.

Meanwhile, melt the remaining butter in a heavy saucepan and mix in the flour. Remove the pan from the heat and carefully stir in the stock and the reserved porcini soaking liquid. Add the wine. Cook, stirring, for 10 minutes. Stir in the mustard. Pour over the mushrooms and blend together well. Toss with hot pasta, season, and sprinkle with Parmesan.

SUMMER SAUCE

This low-calorie sauce is full of natural goodness. Try it with farfalle or spaghetti, and a crisp green salad.

• Make well in advance of serving so the flavors have time to blend.

2 1/4 pounds ripe plum tomatoes, peeled
(see page 17), seeded, and chopped
6 tablespoons extra virgin olive oil
1/2 tablespoon chopped fresh oregano
2 tablespoons chopped fresh basil

2 tablespoons chopped fresh parsley
2 tablespoons chopped black olives
2 cloves garlic, peeled and minced
1/2 teaspoon sugar
Salt and freshly ground black pepper

Put all the ingredients in a large bowl and mix together well. Let the sauce stand at room temperature for at least 2 hours, then season and toss with hot pasta.

SPICY HERB SAUCE

This delicious sauce has a spicy, Middle-Eastern flavor. Serve with penne or macaroni, and a lettuce and cucumber salad.

1/4 cup olive oil
2 cloves garlic, peeled and minced
1 onion, minced
2 tablespoons chopped fresh parsley
2 tablespoons chopped fresh mint

1/2 teaspoon ground cinnamon
1 tablespoon lemon juice
Salt and freshly ground black pepper
1 tablespoon chopped fresh cilantro
1-2 tablespoons pine nuts, toasted (see page 17)

Heat the oil in a heavy-based pan and fry the garlic and onion for 5 minutes or until golden. Add the parsley, mint, cinnamon, and lemon juice and mix together well. Season, toss with hot pasta, and sprinkle with cilantro and pine nuts.

• This sauce can also be served with cold pasta.

RED ONION AND BLACK OLIVE SAUCE

This colorful sauce has a delicate flavor, tinged with a mild sweetness. Try it with fettuccine, linguine, or spaghetti, and a watercress salad.

1/4 cup olive oil
2 red onions, halved and sliced
1 teaspoon sugar
3 tablespoons balsamic vinegar

2 heaping tablespoons pitted
black olives, halved
Salt and freshly ground pepper
1 tablespoon butter
1 tablespoon chopped fresh parsley

Heat the oil in a heavy-based pan and stir in the onions to coat them with oil, then sprinkle with the sugar and cook for 5 minutes or until translucent. Add the vinegar and olives, season, and simmer for a further 2 minutes.

Remove from the heat and stir in the butter. Sprinkle with parsley, then check the seasoning and toss with hot pasta.

• This sauce can also be served with cold pasta.

PEA, PANCETTA, AND CREAM SAUCE

This is a light, refreshing sauce where each flavor comes through individually. Try it with fusilli or spaghetti.

1 tablespoon olive oil
1 thick slice pancetta, diced
1 onion, minced
1 clove garlic, peeled and minced
3/4 pound (2 1/2 cups) frozen green peas

1 1/2 cups heavy cream
1/2 ounce fresh basil leaves, torn in strips
(about 1/3 cup loosely packed)
Salt and freshly ground black pepper
Freshly grated Parmesan cheese

Heat the oil in a heavy-based pan and fry the pancetta for 1 minute. Add the onion and garlic and fry until soft, 3–4 minutes.

Meanwhile, cook the peas in a pan of boiling salted water. Drain, and add to the pancetta mixture. Then pour in the cream and simmer for 5 minutes.

Stir in the basil and season. Toss with hot pasta and sprinkle with Parmesan.

TOMATO, ARUGULA, AND BASIL SAUCE

This is a classic combination of fresh summer ingredients. Serve with a tubular pasta such as rigatoni or penne.

• This sauce needs to stand for at least 2-3 hours to enhance the flavors.

6 tablespoons extra virgin olive oil
1 pound ripe tomatoes, peeled (see page 17),
seeded, and roughly chopped
1 1/2 ounces arugula, roughly chopped
(about 3/4 cup)

1 tablespoon roughly chopped fresh basil
4 cloves garlic, peeled and minced
1/2 teaspoon sugar
1/2 teaspoon red wine vinegar
Salt and freshly ground black pepper

Combine all the ingredients in a large bowl and let stand at room temperature for 2–3 hours.

Toss with hot pasta and serve.

• This sauce can also be served with cold pasta.

BROCCOLI AND TOASTED BREAD CRUMB SAUCE

A tasty combination of ingredients with a lovely crunchy topping. Excellent with conchiglie or fusilli.

1 pound small broccoli florets
1/4 cup extra virgin olive oil
3 cloves garlic, peeled and crushed
with a garlic press
1 cup dry bread crumbs

1/2 cup freshly grated Parmesan cheese,
plus more for serving
1 tablespoon lemon juice
Salt and freshly ground pepper
2 tablespoons pine nuts, toasted (see page 17)

Steam the broccoli until tender, 3–4 minutes, then set aside in a warm bowl.

Heat the oil in a heavy-based pan and fry the garlic for 30 seconds. Add the bread crumbs and Parmesan and, stirring constantly, fry for 2–3 minutes or until crunchy and golden.

Sprinkle the broccoli with lemon juice, then top with the bread-crumb mixture. Season and sprinkle with more Parmesan and the pine nuts. Toss with hot pasta and serve.

Right: Roasted Vegetable Sauce

LEEK, PROSCIUTTO, AND CREAM SAUCE

The distinctive flavor of prosciutto goes well with the more delicate flavors of leeks and cream. Try it with spaghetti or linguine.

2 sticks (1 cup) unsalted butter	1 1/4 cups heavy cream
5 medium-sized leeks, cut in 1/2-inch slices	3/4 cup chicken stock, preferably homemade
4 shallots, sliced	1 1/2 ounces prosciutto, cut in strips
4 cloves garlic, peeled and crushed	Salt and freshly ground black pepper
with a garlic press	2 tablespoons chopped fresh parsley

Melt the butter in a heavy-based pan. Add the leeks, shallots, and garlic and cook for 5 minutes or until soft.

Stir in the cream, stock, and prosciutto and bring to a boil, then lower the heat and simmer gently for 20 minutes. Season, add the parsley, and toss with hot pasta.

LIMA BEAN AND HAM SAUCE

This is a colorful, full-bodied sauce with a wonderful texture. Serve with penne or spaghetti.

2 tablespoons olive oil	2 stalks celery, chopped
4 thick slices smoked bacon, diced	1 pound frozen lima beans
1 onion, chopped	1/4 pound cooked ham, cut in strips
2 cloves garlic, peeled and crushed	3 tablespoons chopped fresh parsley
with a garlic press	Salt and freshly ground black pepper

Heat the oil in a heavy-based pan and cook the bacon, onion, garlic, and celery gently for 10–12 minutes. Pour off excess fat.

Meanwhile, cook the lima beans in a pan of boiling salted water until tender. Drain, and add to the vegetables. Stir in the ham, then sprinkle with parsley, season, and toss with hot pasta.

PASTA SALAD WITH SPRING VEGETABLES

The sauce for this attractive salad is deliciously tangy. Just the thing for a hot summer's day.

1/4 pound fusilli	1 1/4 cups crème fraîche
1 tablespoon olive oil	2 tablespoons cream-style horseradish
3 ounces asparagus tips	1 tablespoon lemon juice
1/2 cup green peas, shelled (fresh or frozen)	Salt and freshly ground black pepper
1 small head of broccoli, cut in small florets	2 heaping tablespoons chopped fresh chives

Cook the pasta, drain, and put in a large bowl. Toss with the olive oil and put to one side.

Steam the vegetables for 4 minutes, then refresh with cold water to keep the color.

Combine the crème fraîche, horseradish, and lemon juice in a bowl. Add to the pasta, season, and mix well. Gently toss in the vegetables and sprinkle with chopped chives.

• Try lima beans in place of peas.

• For extra color, throw in a handful of pitted black olives.

• A little fresh mint, coarsely chopped, is delicious mixed into the salad.

• This sauce is best served at room temperature—do not keep it in the refrigerator.

FRESH BEET SAUCE

This colorful sauce looks amazing with a beet-based pasta.

5 medium-sized beets, cooked,	Juice of 1/2 lemon
peeled, and cut in cubes	TO FINISH
6 tablespoons virgin olive oil	Salt and freshly ground black pepper
2 heaping tablespoons fresh basil	2 ounces Parmesan cheese, freshly cut in shavings
leaves torn in pieces	

Toss all the ingredients with hot or cold pasta, season, and sprinkle with Parmesan shavings.

FENNEL AND PANCETTA SAUCE

The distinctive flavors of pancetta and fennel complement each other to perfection. Serve with brandelle or maltagliati.

1 tablespoon olive oil	1/2 ounce fresh basil leaves, torn in strips
2 fennel bulbs, outer leaves removed, sliced	(about 1/3 cup)
1 onion, sliced	1 tablespoon lemon juice
3 tablespoons chopped pancetta	Salt and freshly ground black pepper
2 1/4 pounds ripe tomatoes, peeled	A few strips of basil for garnish
(see page 17), seeded, and chopped	

Heat the olive oil in a heavy-based pan and sauté the fennel, onion, and pancetta for 6 minutes. Add the tomatoes and basil and cook until soft, 3–4 minutes. Stir in the lemon juice, season, sprinkle with basil, and toss with hot pasta.

Right: Red Onion and Black Olive Sauce

Above: Zucchini, Garlic, and Toasted Bread Crumb Sauce

EGGPLANT SAUCE

This refreshing sauce has a delicate flavor. Try it with pappardelle or large tagliatelle.

• The eggplant needs an hour's preparation before you start cooking the sauce.

1 large eggplant, peeled and sliced	1 tablespoon lemon juice
Salt	2 tablespoons pine nuts, toasted (see page 17)
1/4 cup olive oil	2 tablespoons sunflower seeds, toasted
2 cloves garlic, peeled and crushed with a garlic press	(see page 17)
2 tablespoons sun-dried tomato paste	1 teaspoon dried hot red pepper flakes
5 tomatoes, peeled (see page 17), seeded, and chopped	Salt and freshly ground black pepper
3 sun-dried tomatoes, reconstituted in warm water or drained of oil, then cut in strips	1/4 cup chopped fresh cilantro

Sprinkle the eggplant slices with salt and let them sweat for 1 hour. Then dry and dice.

Heat the olive oil in a heavy-based pan and fry the garlic for 30 seconds. Stir in the sun-dried tomato paste and then the eggplant dice and cook gently until tender but not mushy, about 1 minute. Add the tomatoes, sun-dried tomatoes, lemon juice, pine nuts, seeds, and hot pepper flakes and mix together well. Season, and cook for 5 minutes.

Sprinkle with cilantro, then toss with hot pasta.

• This sauce can be served with cold pasta.

SPINACH SAUCE

Try this light creamy sauce with festoni or pappardelle.

1 ounce spinach leaves, washed and tough stems removed	1/4 cup flour
2 tablespoons butter	1 cup milk
1 clove garlic, peeled and crushed with a garlic press	1/8 teaspoon freshly grated nutmeg
	2 tablespoons freshly grated Parmesan cheese
	Salt and freshly ground black pepper

Cook the spinach for 4–5 minutes. Press out excess liquid, but reserve 2 tablespoons of the liquid.

Melt the butter in a small saucepan, add the garlic, and cook for 30 seconds. Add the flour and stir to a paste. Still stirring, pour in the milk a little at a time. Bring to a boil and simmer for 2–3 minutes, stirring occasionally. Add the nutmeg, spinach, reserved spinach liquid, and Parmesan, then transfer the mixture to a food processor and blend for 30 seconds. Season and toss with hot pasta.

ZUCCHINI, GARLIC, AND TOASTED BREAD CRUMB SAUCE

This sauce not only tastes good but smells wonderful too! Try it with farfalle or fusilli.

5 tablespoons olive oil	Salt and freshly ground black pepper
3 cloves garlic, peeled and minced	1/3 cup dry bread crumbs
1 pound zucchini, diced	2 tablespoons freshly grated Parmesan cheese

Heat 3 tablespoons of the oil in a heavy-based pan, add 2 cloves of garlic and the zucchini, and season. Toss until the zucchini begin to soften around the edges. Remove and drain on paper towels.

Add the remaining oil to the pan and gently fry the bread crumbs with the remaining garlic until they turn golden, about 1 minute. Return the zucchini to the pan and gently fry for 1 minute, stirring well. Season, toss with hot pasta, and sprinkle with Parmesan.

YELLOW PEPPER BUTTER SAUCE

This is a smooth, sophisticated sauce with a delicate flavor. Delicious with fettuccine, and an arugula salad.

8 yellow bell peppers, peeled (see page 17)	Salt and freshly ground black pepper
2 sticks (1 cup) salted butter, cut in chunks	1 heaping tablespoon fresh basil leaves torn in strips

Place the peppers and butter in a food processor and blend until smooth. Transfer the mixture to a small saucepan and heat gently for 3–4 minutes. Season, toss with hot pasta, and sprinkle with basil.

ROASTED VEGETABLE SAUCE

This gutsy vegetable sauce is topped with melted mozzarella. Serve with penne, gnocchetti rigati, or conchiglie, and a crisp green salad.

Preheat the oven to 450°F.

2 zucchini, cut in 1-inch cubes	*3 cloves garlic, peeled and chopped*
1 pound large ripe tomatoes, halved or cut into rough slices, depending on the size of the tomato	*½ ounce fresh basil leaves, roughly chopped (about ⅓ cup)*
1 red bell pepper, cut in rough slices	*Salt and freshly ground black pepper*
1 yellow bell pepper, cut in rough slices	*¼ cup extra virgin olive oil*
2 small eggplants, cut in rough slices	*¼ pound mozzarella cheese, shredded*
	5 leaves fresh basil, torn in strips

Spread the vegetables in a large shallow baking pan and sprinkle with the garlic, chopped basil, salt, and pepper. Sprinkle the oil over the vegetables and mix well to ensure they are evenly coated. Roast for 30 minutes.

Remove the pan from the oven and sprinkle the mozzarella and basil strips over the hot vegetables. Toss with hot pasta, season, and serve.

• This sauce can also be served with cold pasta.

PUTTANESCA SAUCE

Originating in the back streets of Naples, this gutsy sauce is wonderful with spaghetti, bucatini, or penne rigate.

2 tablespoons extra virgin olive oil	*2 tablespoons tomato paste*
2 cloves garlic, peeled and minced	*1 tablespoon capers, rinsed and drained*
10 large leaves fresh basil, chopped	*1 pound ripe tomatoes, peeled (see page 17), seeded, and chopped*
1 fresh hot red chili pepper, seeded and minced	*Salt and freshly ground black pepper*
1 can (2 ounces) anchovies, drained	*Freshly grated Parmesan cheese*
1 ⅓ cups roughly chopped black olives	

Heat the oil in a heavy-based pan and gently fry the garlic, basil, and chili for 1 minute—take care not to burn the garlic. Add the remaining ingredients, season, and simmer for 45 minutes, stirring occasionally.

Toss with hot pasta and sprinkle with Parmesan.

FLAGEOLET BEAN AND HAM SAUCE

A strong-flavored rustic sauce. Try it with bucatini or spaghetti.

• Put the beans in water to soak the night before.

1 cup dried flageolet beans, soaked overnight	*1 tablespoon chopped fresh rosemary*
¼ cup olive oil	*1 teaspoon dried hot red pepper flakes*
¼ pound cooked ham, cut in fine strips	*2 tablespoons dry white wine*
2 cloves garlic, chopped	*¾ cup freshly grated pecorino romano cheese*
1 tablespoon chopped fresh parsley	*Salt and freshly ground black pepper*
1 tablespoon chopped fresh sage	

Drain the beans, then cook in boiling salted water until tender, about 1 hour. Drain and set aside.

Heat the oil in a heavy-based skillet and fry the ham, garlic, herbs, and hot pepper flakes for 5 minutes. Add the beans and wine and cook for a further 6–7 minutes, stirring occasionally. If the mixture becomes too dry, add a little more wine or water.

Stir in the cheese, season, and toss with hot pasta.

WILTED ARUGULA AND PARMESAN SAUCE

The unique flavor of arugula is accentuated when it is cooked. Once tried, this sauce will become a favorite! Serve with linguine or spaghetti.

2 tablespoons virgin olive oil
1 clove garlic, peeled and crushed
with a garlic press
¼ pound arugula leaves

Salt and freshly ground black pepper
1 ounce Parmesan cheese, freshly
cut in shavings

Gently heat the oil in a heavy-based pan over a medium heat, add the garlic, and fry until pale golden, about 30 seconds. Remove the garlic with a slotted spoon and discard. Add the arugula and toss around to ensure all the leaves are coated with garlic-flavored oil, then cook for 1 minute or until soft.

Toss with hot pasta, season, and stir in the Parmesan.

TOMATO SAUCE

An all-time classic! There's no substitute for a really tasty tomato sauce. Serve with any kind of pasta, and a crisp green salad.

1 tablespoon olive oil
1–2 cloves garlic, peeled and crushed
with a garlic press
1 pound ripe tomatoes, peeled (see page 17)
and chopped, or 2 cans (16 ounces each)
tomatoes, drained and chopped
1 teaspoon sugar

1 tablespoon chopped fresh parsley
1 tablespoon chopped fresh basil
Salt and freshly ground black pepper
1 teaspoons tomato paste
2 tablespoons red wine
Freshly grated Parmesan cheese

Heat the oil in a saucepan and fry the garlic for 30 seconds. Add the tomatoes, sugar, and herbs, then season. Simmer for 10 minutes. Add the tomato paste and wine and simmer for a further 15 minutes or until the sauce thickens and sweetens—taste to check.

Season, toss with hot pasta, and sprinkle with Parmesan.

• This recipe makes just under a quart of sauce.

• This sauce can also be served with cold pasta.

FISH SAUCES

All recipes are for four people.

TUNA, LEMON, AND CAPER SAUCE

A last-minute supper dish. Serve with farfalle, plus a salad of tomatoes and black olives.

1/2 cup heavy cream
2 tablespoons lemon juice
1 clove garlic, peeled and crushed
with a garlic press
1 can (7 ounces) tuna, drained

3 tablespoons chopped fresh flat-leaf parsley
2 teaspoons capers, drained and rinsed
1/4 teaspoon cayenne pepper
Freshly ground black pepper
1 lemon, cut in wedges

Put the cream, lemon juice, and garlic in a food processor and blend for 30 seconds. Transfer the mixture to a bowl, add the tuna, 2 tablespoons of the parsley, and the capers, and mix together well. Sprinkle with the cayenne and black pepper.

Toss with hot pasta, then sprinkle with the remaining parsley and decorate with wedges of lemon.

CAVIAR AND CREME FRAICHE SAUCE

For the unashamedly indulgent! This sophisticated combination can be served with a delicate pasta, such as fresh linguine or fettuccine.

1/3 cup crème fraîche
1/3 cup chopped fresh chives

Freshly ground black pepper
4 ounces salmon roe caviar

Put the crème fraîche and chives in a heavy-based saucepan and gently warm over a low heat. Remove from the heat and season with pepper.

Toss with hot pasta and top each serving with a spoonful of caviar.

• This sauce can also be served with cold fusilli or farfalle.

SHRIMP, GARLIC, AND CREAM SAUCE

Full of flavor, this rich sauce is perfect for a dinner party. Serve with farfalle or fusilli, and a spinach and tomato salad.

3 tablespoons heavy cream
6 ounces cream cheese mixed with
1 crushed clove of garlic and
1 tablespoon finely chopped chives

6 ounces small cooked peeled shrimp
1 tablespoon chopped fresh parsley
1 teaspoon grated lemon zest
Freshly ground black pepper

Heat the cream and cheese in a heavy-based saucepan over a low heat, stirring constantly. As soon as the mixture is smooth, turn up the heat and bring to a boil. Remove from the heat and stir in the rest of the ingredients.

Toss with hot pasta and serve.

SMOKED SALMON AND WHISKY SAUCE

Just the thing for an impromptu dinner. Serve with farfalle, and an arugula salad.

6 tablespoons butter
1/2 pound smoked salmon,
cut in small strips
1–2 teaspoons Scotch whisky
(no more—it can be overpowering)

1/2 cup crème fraîche
Freshly ground black pepper

Melt the butter in a heavy-based pan over a medium heat and toss the salmon for a few seconds. Almost immediately stir in the whisky followed by the crème fraîche.

Season with pepper and toss with hot pasta.

SPICY FISH SAUCE

This strong-flavored sauce looks and tastes wonderful. Serve with bucatini, and a crisp green salad.

2 cans (16 ounces each) chopped tomatoes
1/3 cup roughly chopped fresh parsley,
plus more for garnish
1 tablespoon chopped fresh dill
1 small fresh hot chili pepper, seeded
and minced
3 cloves garlic, peeled and roughly chopped
1 fish bouillon cube, dissolved in
7 tablespoons hot water

2 tablespoons Pernod
Salt and freshly ground black pepper
1 pound mixed seafood: squid cut in
1/2-inch rings, monkfish cut in 10-inch cubes,
and large shrimp in their shells
(shells add flavor) or peeled

Put all the ingredients except the seafood in a food processor and blend for 1 minute. Pour into a saucepan, bring to a boil, and simmer for 10 minutes. Add the seafood and cook for a further 4 minutes. Toss with hot pasta and sprinkle with parsley.

• If any of the recommended seafood is unavailable, substitute with a firm-fleshed white fish.

• For the ultimate indulgence, add chunks of fresh lobster.

CRAB AND GINGER SAUCE

The delicate flavor of crab is sharpened by the addition of ginger. Delicious with fusilli or farfalle, and a Napa cabbage salad.

10 tablespoons butter
Small bunch green onions, trimmed and chopped
3- to 4-inch piece fresh gingerroot, peeled and grated
1 cup heavy cream
1 tablespoon sherry
1/4 cup dry white wine
Salt and freshly ground black pepper
6 ounces white crabmeat, flaked
1 tablespoon chopped fresh cilantro

Melt the butter in a heavy-based saucepan and fry the green onions and ginger until golden. Pour on the cream, sherry, and wine, season, and stir well. Bring to a boil and cook until the sauce thickens, about 5 minutes. Stir in the crabmeat.

Toss with hot pasta and sprinkle with cilantro.

CLAM SAUCE

One of the best—a classic from Naples. Excellent with spaghetti or tagliolini, and a fennel salad dressed with extra virgin olive oil and fresh lemon juice.

3 tablespoons olive oil
3 cloves garlic, peeled and chopped
4 large ripe tomatoes, peeled (see page 17), seeded, and chopped
1 pound canned clams, drained, or 3 pounds small fresh hardshell clams, in their shells, well scrubbed
Salt and freshly ground black pepper
3 tablespoons chopped fresh parsley

Heat the oil in a heavy-based pan and sauté the garlic for 30 seconds. Add the tomatoes and cook for 5 minutes, stirring occasionally. Stir in the clams. If using canned clams, cook for a further 2 minutes. If using fresh clams, cook for 5 minutes or until the shells are all open (discard any that remain closed).

Season, toss with hot pasta, and sprinkle with parsley.

• This sauce can also be served with cold pasta.

ANCHOVY, RED PEPPER, AND CHILI SAUCE

An aromatic sauce with a good, strong flavor. Try it with conchiglie, or serve as an antipasto.

Preheat the oven to 400°F.

5 red bell peppers
1/2 cup olive oil
3 cloves garlic, peeled and crushed with a garlic press
1 fresh hot red chili pepper, minced
2 cans (2 ounces each) anchovies, drained
1/3 cup chopped fresh parsley
Freshly ground black pepper
Freshly grated Parmesan cheese

Put the bell peppers on a baking sheet and roast for 25–30 minutes or until their skins turn black. Put them in a plastic bag, seal, and let cool. Then, over a bowl, peel, seed, and cut into 1/2-inch strips. Reserve the juices.

Heat the oil in a heavy-based pan and sauté the garlic and chili over a medium heat for 1 minute. Add the bell peppers with any reserved juices and the anchovies and sauté for a further 2–3 minutes. Stir in the parsley and season with pepper. Toss with hot pasta and sprinkle with Parmesan.

• This sauce can also be served with cold pasta, but leave out the Parmesan.

SCALLOPS WITH BLACK PASTA

Serve the scallops with black ink pasta and a fresh green salad to create an eye-catching effect.

2 tablespoons light olive oil
12 large sea scallops, sliced in half horizontally
1 1/4 cups dry white vermouth
1–2 teaspoons balsamic vinegar
Salt and freshly ground black pepper
1 tablespoon butter
2 tablespoons chopped fresh flat-leaf parsley

Pour the oil into a very hot pan and quickly fry the scallops on both sides until golden but not quite cooked. Remove and set aside in a warm dish.

Add the wine to the pan and stir and scrape to mix with the residue from the scallops. Bring the liquid to a boil and simmer until reduced by about half the original quantity. Add the vinegar and season, then return the scallops to the pan and cook for 1 minute. Gently stir in the butter. Pour the sauce over hot pasta and sprinkle with parsley.

SCALLOPS WITH STIR-FRIED RATATOUILLE

The flavor of fresh scallops blends beautifully with a ratatouille of fresh vegetables. Serve with tagliatelle.

12 sea scallops
¹/₄ cup olive oil
Salt and freshly ground black pepper
1 clove garlic, peeled and crushed with a garlic press
1 small red onion, cut in thin slices
1 red bell pepper, cut in very thin strips
1 eggplant, thinly sliced and cut in ¹/₄ x 2-inch strips

3 zucchini, thinly sliced and cut in ¹/₄ x 2-inch strips
1 wineglass dry white wine
1 tablespoon tomato paste
10 leaves fresh basil, chopped
Juice of 1 large lemon

Lightly brush the scallops with olive oil, season with a little black pepper, and set aside.

Heat the remaining oil in a heavy-based, deep-sided pan and gently sauté the garlic, onion, and red pepper. When the mixture begins to soften, add the eggplant and zucchini. Season, and cook until the vegetables are tender but not mushy, 4–5 minutes. Pour in the wine, then add tomato paste and basil and stir well. Keep hot.

Heat a heavy-based skillet until it starts to smoke. Throw in the scallops and brown them lightly on both sides, then lower the heat and cook for 3–4 minutes, turning once or twice to ensure they cook evenly.

Toss the ratatouille with hot pasta and serve with the scallops on top. Squeeze lemon juice over the dish and serve.

SEAFOOD SAUCE

Just the sauce for a hot summer day. Serve with farfalle or conchiglie.

¹/₂ pound pasta, cooked
¹/₂ pound mixed cooked shellfish: shrimp, mussels, squid, and clams
¹/₂ pound sugar snap peas, cooked for 2–3 minutes
2 baby gherkins or cornichons, chopped
3 tablespoons chopped fresh basil

2 tablespoons chopped fresh parsley
1 teaspoon dried thyme or oregano
6 tablespoons olive oil
1 tablespoon lemon juice
Salt and freshly ground black pepper
1 tablespoon capers, drained

Mix the pasta with the shellfish, sugar snap peas, and gherkins.

In a separate bowl combine the herbs, olive oil, and lemon juice. Toss with the pasta. Season and sprinkle with capers.

Above: *Scallops with Black Pasta*

SQUID AND TOMATO SAUCE

This richly satisfying sauce has a slightly Asian flavor. Serve with spaghetti or any long, round pasta.

¹/₃ cup olive oil
1 clove garlic, peeled and crushed with a garlic press
1 small fresh hot red chili pepper, seeded and minced
2 pounds ripe tomatoes, peeled (see page 17), seeded, and minced

1 pound squid, cleaned and cut in rings (leave the tentacles whole)
Salt and freshly ground black pepper
2–3 tablespoons chopped fresh cilantro

Heat the oil in a heavy-based pan and sauté the garlic and chili for 30 seconds. Add the tomatoes and simmer for 5 minutes, stirring occasionally. Then add the squid and simmer for a further 2 minutes.

Season, stir in the cilantro, and toss with hot pasta.

SQUID, WINE, AND HERB SAUCE

Wonderfully fishy and garlicky, this is an excellent sauce to serve with ink vermicelli or tagliolini.

2 tablespoons olive oil
1 small onion, chopped
1/2 cup chopped fresh flat-leaf parsley
3 cloves garlic, peeled and chopped
1 pound squid, cleaned and cut in rings (leave the tentacles whole)

2 wineglasses red wine
2 1/2 cups good fish stock
Salt and freshly ground black pepper
2 tablespoons chopped fresh basil
2 tablespoons chopped fresh chives

Heat the oil in a heavy-based pan over a medium heat and sauté the onion until soft. Add the parsley and garlic and cook for 1 minute, stirring occasionally. Put in the squid, turn up the heat, and sauté for 2 minutes, then lower the heat, add the wine and fish stock, and simmer very gently until the squid is tender, 1–1 1/2 hours.

Toss with hot pasta, season, and sprinkle with basil and chives.

SHRIMP, SNOW PEA, AND FRESH MINT SAUCE

Minty, creamy, and crunchy, try this delicious sauce with tortiglioni or penette.

2 tablespoons olive oil
2 cloves garlic, peeled and chopped
6 ounces snow peas
3/4 pound small shelled shrimp

3 tablespoons chopped fresh mint leaves
3/4 cup crème fraîche
Salt and freshly ground black pepper

Gently heat the oil in a saucepan, add the garlic and snow peas, and cook for 1 minute. Add the remaining ingredients, season, and cook for another minute, then toss with hot pasta.

• To serve cold, replace the crème fraîche with plain yogurt, stirring this into the sauce once it has cooled.

LOBSTER AND CHEESE SAUCE

This sauce has a subtle fishy flavor. Try it with fettuccine or spaghetti.

1 tablespoon olive oil
1 tablespoon chopped onion
1 wineglass dry white wine
2 heaping tablespoons crème fraîche
2 ounces (1/4 cup) cream cheese with garlic and herbs

1-pound cooked lobster, meat removed and cut in 1/2-inch pieces
1 tablespoon chopped fresh chives
1 tablespoon fresh basil leaves torn in strips
1 tablespoon chopped fresh parsley
Salt and freshly ground black pepper

Heat the oil in a heavy-based pan and sauté the onion until soft but not brown. Pour in the wine and simmer for 4 minutes. Add the crème fraîche and cheese and bring to a boil, stirring. Simmer until the sauce starts to thicken, then add the lobster meat and heat for 1 minute.

Stir in the herbs, season, and toss with hot pasta.

TUNA, TOMATO, AND BLACK OLIVE SAUCE

Bursting with Mediterranean flavors, this sauce is delicious with penne, and a salad of dandelion leaves.

6 tablespoons olive oil
1 red onion, minced
3 cloves garlic, peeled and chopped
1 sprig fresh thyme
1 can (16 ounces) crushed tomatoes
2 tablespoons thinly sliced sun-dried tomatoes, reconstituted in warm water or drained of oil
1 heaping tablespoon chopped pitted black olives

1 teaspoon green peppercorns packed in brine, drained and chopped
1 can (7 ounces) tuna, drained
1 can (16 ounces) cannelini beans, drained and roughly chopped
Grated zest of 1 lemon
Salt and freshly ground black pepper
1/4 cup chopped fresh parsley

Heat the oil in a heavy-based, deep-sided pan and sauté the onion with the garlic and thyme until soft. Then turn up the heat, add the canned tomatoes with their juice, and cook until the sauce thickens, stirring occasionally. Turn down the heat, stir in the sun-dried tomatoes, olives, peppercorns, tuna, beans, and lemon zest, and cook for a further 2 minutes.

Toss with hot pasta, season, and sprinkle with parsley.

• This sauce can also be served with cold pasta.

TUNA , NUT, CAPER, AND LEMON SAUCE

This sauce has a slightly sharp edge and a lovely nutty texture. Serve with a green leaf salad.

• The sauce needs to marinate overnight.

Preheat the oven to 350°F.

2 pounds fresh tuna
5 tablespoons olive oil
2/3 cup pine nuts, toasted (see page 17)
2 cloves garlic, peeled and crushed with a garlic press
2 tablespoons capers, drained and roughly chopped

1/2 teaspoon dried hot red pepper flakes
Grated zest and juice of 2 lemons
2 tablespoons chopped fresh basil leaves
Salt and freshly ground black pepper

Lightly brush the fish with 1 tablespoon of the olive oil and wrap in foil, sealing tightly. Bake for 10–15 minutes, then remove, let cool, and flake.

Combine the flaked fish with the remaining ingredients in a bowl and mix well. Marinate at room temperature overnight.

Toss with hot pasta and season.

• This sauce can also be served with cold pasta.

Salmon, Olive, and Bean Sauce

A surprisingly gutsy, full-flavored sauce that goes well with festone and maltagliati.

Preheat the oven to 375°F.

¹/2 pound salmon fillet
1 can (16 ounces) flageolet beans
¹/2 cup chopped black olives

5 tablespoons extra virgin olive oil
Salt and freshly ground black pepper

Lightly oil an ovenproof dish, put in the salmon, and bake for 10 minutes. Remove, let cool, and flake.

Heat the beans in their liquid. Drain and put into a large bowl with the salmon and remaining ingredients. Toss with hot pasta, season, and add another dash of extra virgin olive oil.

Oyster and Champagne Sauce

The extravagant combination of oysters and champagne is unbeatable! Serve with capelli d'angelo or linguini.

2 tablespoons butter
2 leeks, finely sliced
1 cup champagne
2 dozen oysters, shucked

1 cup crème fraîche
Salt and freshly ground black pepper
1 tablespoon chopped fresh chives

Melt the butter in a large, heavy-based pan. Add the leeks and sauté for 2–3 minutes. Pour in the champagne and heat until the liquid starts to simmer. Add the oysters and cook for 2 minutes, then remove them with a slotted spoon and set aside. Simmer the champagne mixture for 6–7 minutes, then stir in the crème fraîche, season, and cook for a further 10 minutes.

Lower the heat, replace the oysters in the sauce, and heat for 30 seconds only. Toss with hot pasta and sprinkle with chives.

• Serve in bowls as the sauce may be a little runny.

• Use Sauternes instead of champagne.

Left: Anchovy, Red Pepper, and Chili Sauce

MUSSEL AND SAFFRON CREAM SAUCE

This sophisticated sauce is delicious with spaghettini or tagliolini.

4 threads saffron
1 1/2 cups crème fraîche
4 tablespoons butter
2 shallots, minced
1 cup fish stock, preferably homemade

2 pounds fresh mussels, shells well
scrubbed and beards removed
Salt and freshly ground black pepper
2 tablespoons chopped fresh chives

Mix the saffron with the crème fraîche and leave to one side.

Melt the butter in a large, heavy-based saucepan and sauté the shallots for 2 minutes. Pour in the stock and bring to simmering point. Add the mussels, cover the pan, and cook for about 6 minutes or until all the shells are open (discard any mussels that remain closed). Strain the liquid through a large strainer or colander set in a bowl and discard any empty shells. Put the mussels in another bowl and set aside.

Return the liquid to the pan and boil until reduced by half the original quantity. Stir in the crème fraîche and saffron mixture and boil for a further 10 minutes. Lower the heat, season, and return the mussels to the sauce to heat for 30 seconds. Toss with hot pasta and sprinkle with chives.

SMOKED TROUT, MAYONNAISE, AND DILL SAUCE

This light summer sauce is excellent with conchiglie, and a crisp green salad.

3/4 cup fresh mayonnaise
6 tablespoons vinaigrette dressing
1 tablespoon lemon juice
Salt and freshly ground black pepper

3 tablespoons chopped fresh dill
1/3 cup chopped fresh chives
1/4 cup chopped fresh basil
8 fillets smoked trout

Toss cold cooked pasta with the mayonnaise, then toss again with the vinaigrette and once more with the lemon juice and seasoning. Stir in the chopped herbs, then very carefully fold in the trout, keeping the pieces as large as possible.

ANCHOVY, CREAM, AND LEMON SAUCE

This is a delicate sauce with a slightly piquant flavor. Excellent with tagliolini, and a salad of tomato, spinach, and hard-boiled egg.

1 tablespoon butter
1 can (2 ounces) anchovies,
drained and rinsed
1 onion, minced
1 teaspoon capers, minced

Grated zest and juice of 1 lemon
1 cup crème fraîche
Salt and freshly ground black pepper
2 tablespoons chopped fresh flat-leaf parsley
1/4 teaspoon cayenne pepper

Melt the butter in a heavy-based pan and cook the anchovies over a very low heat, stirring, until they break up, about 4 minutes. Be careful as they burn very easily. Add the onion and cook for 5 minutes, then add the capers and lemon zest and juice and cook for another 5 minutes. Stir in the crème fraîche and cook until the sauce starts to thicken. Remove from the heat and toss with hot pasta. Season, sprinkle with parsley, and dust with a little cayenne pepper.

SALMON, NUTMEG, AND FENNEL SAUCE

The exquisite taste of salmon is accentuated by the subtle combination of fennel and nutmeg. Try it with spaghettini.

Preheat the oven to 375°F.

3/4 pound salmon fillet
1 1/4 cups heavy cream
4 tablespoons butter
1 wineglass dry white wine
1/4 teaspoon freshly grated nutmeg

2–3 tablespoons freshly grated
pecorino romano cheese
1 medium-sized fennel bulb, thinly sliced
Salt and freshly ground black pepper
2 tablespoons chopped parsley

Lightly oil an ovenproof dish, put in the salmon, and bake for 10–12 minutes. Remove, let cool, and flake.

Put the cream, butter, wine, and nutmeg in a heavy-based saucepan and bring to a boil. Add the cheese and fennel, then gently stir in the salmon.

Toss with hot pasta, season, and sprinkle with parsley.

Left: Spicy Fish Sauce

MEAT SAUCES

All recipes are for four people.

Bresaola and green peppercorn sauce

The unusual combination of spicy green peppercorns and the delicate flavor of bresaola is perfect with linguine or fettuccine, and a lamb's lettuce salad.

1 tablespoon butter	*2 ounces bresaola, cut in 1/2-inch strips*
1 clove garlic, peeled and crushed	*1 cup heavy cream*
with a garlic press	*Salt and freshly ground black pepper*
1 1/2 ounces bottled green peppercorns,	
rinsed and drained	

Melt the butter in a saucepan and gently fry the garlic until golden, about 30 seconds. Add the peppercorns and fry them until they pop, 5–6 minutes. Then stir in the bresaola, mixing together well. Pour in the cream, turn up the heat, and slowly bring to a boil, then lower the heat and simmer for 2–3 minutes.

Season and toss with hot pasta.

Hot bacon sauce

This versatile sauce is like a hot vinaigrette dressing. Try it with fusilli or penne.

3/4 cup olive oil	*1/4 cup balsamic vinegar*
3–4 cloves garlic, peeled and crushed	*1 1/2 tablespoons chopped fresh parsley*
with a garlic press	*Salt and freshly ground black pepper*
6 ounces smoked bacon, cut in 1/4-inch strips	*Freshly grated Parmesan cheese*

Heat half the oil in a large, heavy-based skillet and gently sauté the garlic for 30 seconds—take care not to burn it. Remove with a slotted spoon, and discard.

Add the bacon to the pan and fry until crisp, about 4 minutes, then pour away all the fat. Scrape the bottom of the pan to loosen the deposits, add the vinegar, and stir well. Pour in the remaining oil and, when the sauce is hot, add the parsley. Season, toss with hot pasta, and sprinkle with Parmesan.

Bolognese sauce

A robust, strong-flavored sauce. Just the thing to warm you up on a cold, wintery night! Serve with tagliolini or spaghetti.

2 thick slices smoked bacon	*2 tablespoons tomato paste*
1/4 pound chicken livers (optional)	*1 1/4 cups chicken stock,*
2 tablespoons olive oil	*preferably homemade*
1 clove garlic, peeled and crushed	*1 bay leaf*
with a garlic press	*1 sprig fresh thyme*
1 tablespoon chopped onion	*1 tablespoon chopped fresh parsley*
1 tablespoon chopped carrot	*6 fennel seeds*
1 tablespoon chopped celery	*Salt and freshly ground black pepper*
1 pound ground round or chopped steak	*Freshly grated Parmesan cheese*
1 wineglass white wine	

Mince the bacon and chicken livers (if using) in a food processor.

Heat the oil in a deep, heavy-based pan and, stirring frequently, sauté the garlic, onion, celery, and carrot until soft. Add the chicken livers, bacon, and beef and cook for a further 2 minutes, then pour in the wine and add the tomato paste. Stir well and and cook for 2 minutes. Add the chicken stock, herbs, and fennel seeds and let simmer gently for 1 hour.

Season, toss with hot pasta, and sprinkle with Parmesan.

• This is the authentic base for lasagne.

• This sauce freezes well, so make double the quantity and keep some in reserve.

Salami and pepperoni sauce

This gutsy sauce has a lovely tangy edge to it. Delicious with tagliatelle, and a tomato salad mixed with very finely sliced shallots.

1 tablespoon olive oil	*1 tablespoon capers, rinsed and drained*
1 jar (10 ounces) Italian pepperoni,	*1 tablespoon chopped fresh parsley*
drained and cut in strips	*Freshly ground black pepper*
3 ounces salami, cut in 1/2 -inch strips	

Heat the oil in a heavy-based pan. Add the pepperoni and salami and cook gently for 5 minutes, stirring occasionally. Stir in the capers and parsley and season with pepper. Toss with hot pasta and serve.

• This sauce can also be served with cold pasta.

PORK, SAFFRON, AND BASIL SAUCE

The unusual combination of saffron and pork is a great success. Serve with orecchiette or penne rigate.

6 strands saffron
1 1/4 cups chicken stock,
preferably homemade
1/2 cup olive oil
1 onion, minced
2 cloves garlic, peeled and crushed
with a garlic press
6 leaves fresh basil, chopped

3 tablespoons chopped fresh parsley
1 tablespoon chopped fresh cilantro
1/2 pound boned loin of pork, ground
1 teaspoon dried hot red pepper flakes
1 tablespoon tomato paste
1 teaspoon soy sauce
Salt and freshly ground black pepper
6 leaves fresh basil, torn in strips

Mix the saffron with the stock and set aside.

Heat the oil in a deep, heavy-based pan over a medium heat and gently sauté the onion, garlic, chopped basil, parsley, and cilantro. When the onion is soft but not brown, stir in the pork and hot pepper flakes.
As soon as the meat starts to brown, stir in the tomato paste, soy sauce, and saffron mixture. Season and simmer for 3–4 minutes.

Toss with hot pasta and sprinkle with strips of basil.

PANCETTA AND CHILI SAUCE

An ingenious sauce with an unusual combination of ingredients. Serve with penne rigate.

1/4 cup virgin olive oil
1 onion, chopped
1 fresh hot red chili pepper, chopped
6 ounces pancetta, finely sliced
1/2 pound collard greens or other
hearty greens, cut in thin strips

1/2 teaspoon ground cumin
3 medium-sized tomatoes, peeled (see page 17),
seeded, and chopped in 1/2-inch pieces
1/2 teaspoon freshly ground black pepper

Heat the oil in a heavy-based pan over a medium heat and gently sauté the onion, chili, and pancetta for 4–5 minutes. Add the greens and cumin and, stirring constantly, cook for 1 minute. Add the tomatoes and cook for another minute.

Season with black pepper and toss with hot pasta.

Left: Bresaola and Green Peppercorn Sauce

PROSCIUTTO AND GOAT CHEESE SAUCE

This ambrosial concoction is wickedly irresistible! Serve with green noodles.

2 tablespoons light olive oil	*2 ounces prosciutto, finely diced*
2 shallots, minced	*Freshly ground black pepper*
2 tablespoons chicken stock	*Freshly grated pecorino romano cheese*
2 tablespoons dry white wine	
6 ounces goat cheese, any rind removed,	
cut in pieces	

Heat the oil in a heavy-based pan and gently fry the shallots until soft but not brown. Add the stock and wine and then the cheese and mix together well. As soon as the cheese has melted, stir in the prosciutto and season with pepper. Toss with hot pasta and sprinkle with pecorino.

FOIE GRAS AND WILD MUSHROOM SAUCE

Creamy and rich, this sauce is best served with fine egg noodles or farfalle.

• This recipe is for 2 people.

1 ounce dried porcini, or 3 ounces	*2 ounces terrine de foie gras, or 3 ounces*
fresh porcini (cèpes)	*foie gras, chopped*
⁷⁄₈ cup chicken stock, preferably homemade	*Freshly ground black pepper*
2 heaped tablespoons crème fraîche	

If using dried mushrooms, put them in a bowl, cover with water, and let soak for 30 minutes. Remove the mushrooms and set aside; discard the water.

Put the stock and crème fraîche in a heavy-based pan and heat gently. Simmer for 2 minutes or until the cream starts to thicken, then add the mushrooms.

Serve hot pasta on individual plates, place the foie gras on top, and pour the sauce over it. Season and serve immediately.

ITALIAN SAUSAGE SAUCE WITH LENTILS AND SPINACH

A robust, rich sauce with a wonderful aroma. Serve with a tubular pasta such as rigatoni.

¹⁄₂ cup lentilles de Puy or other small lentils	*6 small Italian sausages, pricked*
1 sprig fresh thyme	*1 clove garlic, chopped*
1 bay leaf	*1 pound baby spinach leaves*
2 cloves garlic, crushed with a garlic press	*²⁄₃ cup chicken stock, preferably homemade*
1 wineglass red wine	*1 tablespoon tomato paste*
4 tablespoons olive oil	*Salt and freshly ground black pepper*

Put the lentils in a saucepan and add the thyme, bay leaf, crushed garlic, red wine, and enough unsalted water to cover. Simmer until the lentils are tender, about 30 minutes. Then drain, discard the herbs and set aside.

Meanwhile, heat 2 tablespoons of the oil in a heavy-based skillet and gently fry the sausages until they are browned on all sides and cooked through. Slice and set aside.

In another pan heat the rest of the oil, add the chopped clove of garlic, and sauté for 30 seconds. Then add the spinach, cooked lentils (drained of any excess water), sausage, chicken stock, and tomato paste and cook for 2–3 minutes, stirring well.

Season and toss with hot pasta.

CREAMED PROSCIUTTO SAUCE

Serve this rich and creamy sauce with penne or fusilli, and a Belgian endive and walnut salad.

4 tablespoons butter	*Salt and freshly ground black pepper*
1 onion, minced	*³⁄₄ cup freshly grated Parmesan cheese*
²⁄₃ cup heavy cream	*1 heaping tablespoon chopped fresh parsley*
2 ounces prosciutto or Parma ham in a	
thick piece, chopped in small pieces	

Melt the butter in a large saucepan and gently fry the onion until soft but not brown. Pour in the cream and bring to a boil. Cook for 1 minute. Stirring constantly, add the prosciutto or Parma ham and seasoning, then the cheese.

Toss with hot pasta and sprinkle with parsley.

Right: Foie Gras and Wild Mushroom Sauce

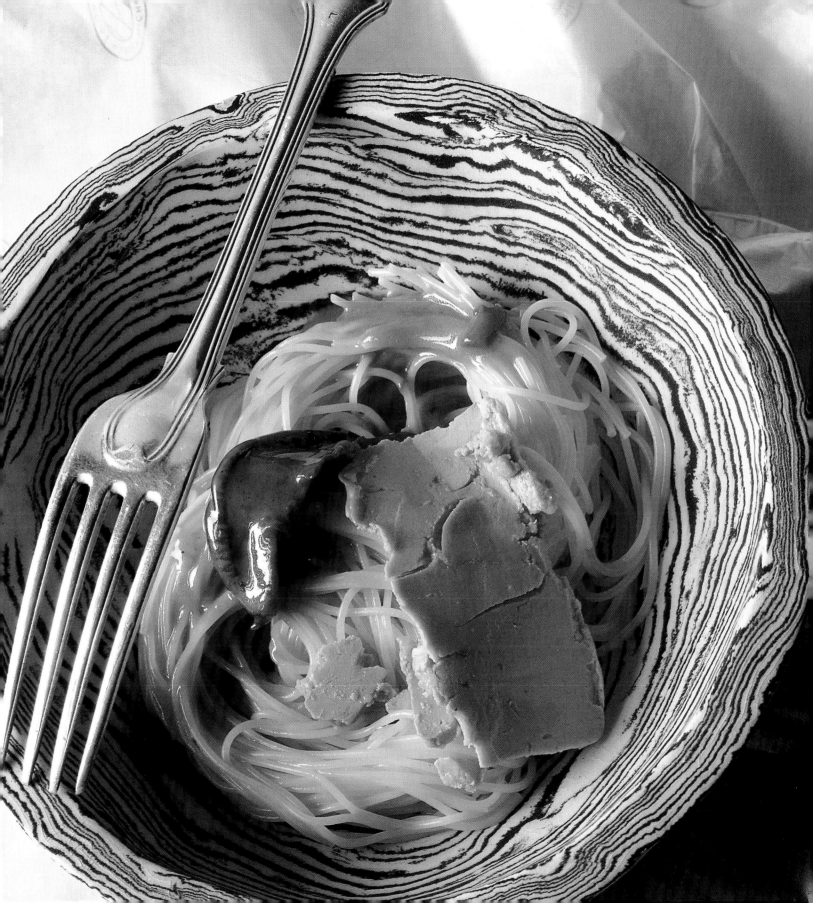

QUAIL, CELERY ROOT, AND MOREL SAUCE

This sophisticated sauce is quick and easy to make. Serve with maltagliati or brandelle.

1 stick (¹/2 cup) butter
1 head celery root, peeled and cut in
¹/4- x 2-inch strips
Breasts of 4 quails (plus livers if obtainable), cut in ¹/4-inch strips

1 oz dried morels, soaked in water for 30 minutes, then rinsed and sliced
¹/4 cup chopped fresh chervil
Salt and freshly ground black pepper
Freshly grated pecorino romano cheese

Heat half of the butter in a heavy-based pan and gently sauté the celery root until it softens, 4–5 minutes. Remove with a slotted spoon to a warm plate.

Turn up the heat and sauté the quail breasts for about 3 minutes. Return the celery root to the pan and add the morels, chervil, and remaining butter. Heat for 2 minutes, stirring occasionally. Then season, toss with hot pasta, and sprinkle with pecorino cheese.

HARE AND BACON SAUCE

This exceptional sauce is worth every minute of the time it takes to make! Serve with pappardelle.

2 tablespoons olive oil
4 tablespoons butter
2 ounces smoked Canadian bacon, chopped
1 small onion, chopped
2 stalks celery, chopped
2 pounds meat from a hare, minced
1 teaspoon chopped fresh thyme

Salt and freshly ground black pepper
1 wineglass dry white wine
1 wineglass red wine
2 cups chicken or veal stock, preferably homemade
Freshly grated Parmesan cheese

Heat the oil and butter in a heavy-based pan over a medium heat and sauté the bacon, onion, and celery until the vegetables are soft. Stir in the meat and thyme and season. As soon as the meat is browned, pour in the wine and simmer until almost completely reduced. Add the stock, then cover and simmer gently for 2–3 hours.

Season, toss with hot pasta, and serve with Parmesan.

SPICY SAUSAGE AND TOMATO SAUCE

This full-bodied sauce has a lovely garlicky flavor. Serve with spaghetti or bucatoni, a spinach and mushroom salad, and Italian bread to mop up the last few drops.

3 tablespoons olive oil
1 small onion, chopped
2 cloves garlic, peeled and crushed with a garlic press
¹/4 cup roughly chopped cooked ham
5 ounces chorizo sausage, skinned and roughly chopped

⁷/8 cup beef stock, preferably homemade
2 ¹/2 cups fresh tomato sauce (see page 41) or 1 can (16 ounces) tomatoes, chopped
2 tablespoons minced fresh parsley
Salt and freshly ground black pepper
Freshly grated Parmesan cheese

Heat the oil in a heavy-based saucepan, add the onion and garlic, and sauté until pale golden. Add the ham and sausage and cook for 3–4 minutes, then add the stock and tomato sauce and simmer for 10–15 minutes, stirring occasionally.

Toss with hot pasta, stir in the parsley, season, and sprinkle with Parmesan.

• For a spicier flavor, add ¹/2 teaspoon dried hot red pepper flakes.

CHICKEN LIVER AND MADEIRA SAUCE

A fabulous combination of ingredients. Serve with conchiglie (large pasta shells), and a salad of lamb's lettuce.

1 tablespoon olive oil
6 ounces chicken livers, chopped
2 ounces thickly sliced smoked Canadian bacon, cut across in thin strips (lardons)

1 clove garlic, peeled and chopped
1 tablespoon chopped fresh tarragon
¹/4 cup madeira
Freshly ground black pepper

Put the oil in a heavy-based pan and quickly fry the livers over a high heat for 1 minute. Add the bacon and garlic and cook for 3–4 minutes, stirring all the time. Add the tarragon and madeira, stir, and cook for another minute.

Toss with hot pasta and season with pepper.

Left: Bolognese Sauce

PORK SAUCE

Traditionally, this might be made with wild boar which probably is unavailable. Serve over pappardelle.

• This sauce needs to marinate overnight or for at least 5 hours, and cook for 1–1 1/2 hours.

1 pound pork loin, cut into 1-inch cubes
(or 1 pound boned loin of wild boar, cut
in cubes)
1/4 cup olive oil
1 onion, minced
1 carrot, minced
1 stalk celery, minced
2 cloves garlic, peeled and crushed
with a garlic press
1 tablespoon tomato paste

2 wineglasses red wine
Salt and freshly ground black pepper
Freshly grated pecorino romano cheese
FOR THE MARINADE
8 juniper berries
1 teaspoon chopped fresh rosemary
2 wineglasses red wine
1 onion, roughly chopped
1/4 cup olive oil

Put the cubes of pork (or boar) in a bowl. Mix together the ingredients for the marinade and pour over the meat. Let marinate overnight or for a minimum of 5 hours. Drain off the marinating liquid, strain, and reserve. (Put the pork in a food processor and chop finely.)

Heat the oil in a heavy-based pan over a medium heat and sauté the meat, onion, carrot, celery, and garlic until the vegetables are soft. Add the wine, marinating liquid, and tomato paste and stir well, then simmer for 1–1 1/2 hours or until the meat is very tender.

Season, toss with hot pasta, and sprinkle with cheese.

Right: *Hot Bacon Sauce*

ACKNOWLEDGMENTS

I would like to thank La Famiglia Restaurant, Loyd Grossman and Orlando Murrin, editor of *Woman & Home*, for donating their delicious recipes.

Also, Rose Prince and Jose Luke for testing the recipes and for their own contributions to the book. Their enthusiasm and energy has been inspirational and they have been a joy to work with. Words cannot describe my admiration for Simon Wheeler's splendid photography. As always, he was enormous fun, and kind and considerate towards the rest of the team.

I would like to thank Elizabeth Gage, Maria Harrington, my son Mark and my assistant Christopher Leach for their enduring support and patience throughout the project.

Last but not least my sincere thanks to the following companies for loaning and supplying food and props for photography: La Picena, Luigi's Delicatessen, Camisa & Son, Taylor & Lake, Harvey & Brockless Ltd, Summerill & Bishop, David Mellor, Verandah, Ceramica Blue, William Yeoward, Designers Guild, Robert Budwig, Lauriance Rogier Antiques, David Pettifer Antiques, Ena Green Antiques, Myriad Antiques, Guinevere Antiques, Clifton Little Venice.

RECIPE INDEX

First published in the United States of America in
1995 by Rizzoli International Publications, Inc.
300 Park Avenue South, New York, NY 10010

First published in Great Britain in 1995 by
George Weidenfeld & Nicolson Limited
The Orion Publishing Group

ISBN 0-8478-1872-1

LC 95-67212

Designed by Thumb Design Partnership

Printed and bound in Italy